Sh
Daughters to Dads

The letters in Clay's heartwarming *Shoebox Letters* collection will make you giggle, will make your eyes tear up and they will, most importantly, inspire you. They will inspire you to be a better parent, to be a better daughter, and just maybe, to write a letter to your own father.

—Rhonda M. Starghill
Director of Membership, Girl Scouts of Western Ohio

"I am pleased to recommend *Shoebox Letters: Daughters to Dads* to readers whose interest in the role of fathers in their daughters' lives has encouraged them to gain insight into this topic. My professional background in the psychology of female personality development as a researcher/author makes me appreciate the contribution of *Shoebox Letters: Daughters to Dads* to men who desire simply-stated principles to help guide them as fathers. Highlighting the personal letters of daughters illustrates these principles and engages the reader in an emotionally meaningful way that makes *Shoebox Letters* an enjoyable as well as instructive book."

—Stephan D. Weiss, PhD., Clinical Psychologist
Research: H.B. Biller and S.D. Weiss
"The father–daughter relationship and the personality development of the female."
Journal of Genetic Psychology, 1970

A wonderful collection of inspiring and moving letters of reflection. These letters are gentle reminders of the values that dads impart—whether intentional or not—by being a dad, and how 'little' moments can have a lasting impact. As a father of young daughters, I found these authentic voices thought provoking, leading me to my own self-reflection, and inspiring me to write a letter to my own father.

—Mark Jeffreys
Founder and Chairman, go Vibrant
Father

Clay has delivered a moment every girl dreams of—discovering a box of old letters and gaining a glimpse into the lives of both writer and recipient. His collection of letters provides inspiring personal insights into the dynamic relationships between dads and daughters, and reading it made me cherish my relationship with my own dad even more!

—Cherylanne Skolnicki
Founder of NourishYourself.com, an online community helping busy, health-conscious women thrive

More Praise

I love my daughters with all my heart. I have done the best I've known how—excelling some days and falling short others. But they have made me a better person and I've learned much through and with them. I've often wished someone had shared a playbook to guide me, to remind me, and to inspire me as a father with the privilege of having two daughters. This is that playbook told through real and heartfelt stories. No matter where you are in your journey as a father and daughter, this book should remind you that every day and every effort is meaningful.

—Marc Connor
    Father of Two Wonderful Daughters
    Chief Marketing Strategist, POSSIBLE

The role a father plays in the life of his daughter is unique and irreplaceable. If you have ever wondered what your daughter is thinking—here it is! In the pages of this book you will find tremendous inspiration to step it up a notch and be an even better father than you are today.

—Matthew Kelly
    Author of The Dream Manager

Shoebox
Letters

Real Letters to Real People…Building Real Relationships

Daughters to Dads

Clay Brizendine

TOTAL HEALTH ORGANIZATION, LLC
CINCINNATI

Shoebox Letters: Daughters to Dads
Real Letters to Real People…Building Real Relationships
Clay Brizendine

ISBN 978-0-9888166-0-2 (paperback)

Publisher:
Total Health Organization, LLC
7672 Montgomery Rd, #156
Cincinnati, OH 45236
www.totalhealthorganization.com

All works republished with consent from the authors.

Design: Chaz DeSimone
          desimonedesign.com

To my wife and daughters.

This book, and this life, wouldn't be possible without you.

Thank you from the bottom of my heart.

And to the writers…

Know that you have my thoughtful and heartfelt thanks

for the heart and soul that you poured

into your letters.

Contents

Foreword

We chose not to find out the sex of our first child at our 20-week appointment. What was done was done, and knowing whether we were having a boy or a girl was something we wanted to wait on. And so we did.

April 16, 2004 was the day that my first daughter was born, but for 10 seconds I wasn't so sure she was a girl. From my vantage point at the top of the bed, the nurse-midwife's call of "It's a Girl!" didn't seem right to me because of an ill-placed umbilical cord. But soon enough, the team of professionals in the room showed me that it was, for sure, a girl, and my thoughts suddenly turned to…Now what?

I had grown up in a testosterone-infused family. I had two younger brothers, 4 of my 5 first cousins were boys, and sports were the norm from the day we were born. Growing up in the '80s, girls had cooties (and maybe they still do—I should ask my kids), and with no female around except Mom, they got little attention in our house until middle school.

In September of 2005, daughter #2 made her way into my family's arms. Not only did she choose to make a bold entrance—false labor 2 days before actual birth, a 90mph trip to the hospital at 2am, and a delivery mere minutes after my wife made it onto a bed—but she chose not to eat the first week of her life. The trips to the hospital and worry for a sick child drove home very readily, if I didn't already know it, that I was a parent.

But a parent of daughters, 16 months apart no less…what was this going to be like? I had brothers and male cousins and boys I hung out with growing up. No one in my family could tell me "Clay, here's what it's like raising girls." So I started doing some research of my own…and what I found was incredible.

My women friends were so interested in talking about, eager to talk about, and ready to talk about their dads that I barely had to ask the question. Many started the conversation with "Oh, I am soooo Daddy's little girl" or "My Dad can do no wrong." I was shocked. Really? I love my dad like no other, but there were *some* things he did wrong. I was fascinated with how boldly women would talk about their dads, how great he was in their eyes, and how long the conversations could really go if I let them.

To be clear, I had friends who have said just the opposite. Their dad wasn't around to do the things that a dad should. I've heard stories of "my dad wanted boys." Divorce crushed the dreams of others. Some dads don't measure up to what we'd like. It can be for a point in time, or it could be a lifetime. As Rocky says in *Rocky Balboa*, "The world ain't all sunshine and rainbows."

Both of these types of stories you'll read about in the following letters. There's as much that can be learned from the stories of less-than-ideal fathers as the stories of those that played the role perfectly.

Shoebox Letters: Daughters to Dads is a project that I've been working on for a long time. Not the book itself, but the stories. The conversations. The memories brought to life in an instant. The emotions: raw, good, and bad.

Over thirty letters in this book are addressed to real life dads from their real life daughters. No editing, no scripting—what you see are the letters themselves in their native form. I did, however, ask them to all start from the same jumping-off point:

"Dad, as I thought about our relationship at this stage of my life, and what your role as my dad truly means to me, I wanted you to know a few things."

Letters from those just starting college. Letters from women executives. A letter from a woman whose father has passed, and two from women whose mothers passed while they were younger. Letters from women whose parents' marriage will last the test of time, and those from homes of divorce. You'll find them all here.

What you'll also find is a degree of anonymity. For some, sharing stories and thoughts about their dad was easy, came naturally, and they didn't care if anyone knew who they were. For others, this was stretching, and it was an exercise that while personal, they wanted to share under the condition of being anonymous. All requests were granted on this front to keep the book as real as possible.

The book's format wrote itself. I didn't set out to create a "Top 10 themes of fatherhood," but amazingly a handful presented themselves such that I almost had no choice but to call them out. You'll see the letters grouped throughout the book within these themes. You'll also notice blank pages at the end of the book. They are there for you to use to turn your own story into your own letter.

I want any man reading this book, whether a current father, father-to-be, or neither, to understand the varying roles that a dad plays in his daughter's life. For most girls and women, their dad is the first male that they love in their life. With that comes amazing responsibility. While the roles of teacher, mentor, coach, friend, etc. all come into play for any dad, they take on special meaning with daughters.

I want any woman reading this book to give herself a chance to reflect, and then maybe to share her own story. Maybe there's a mom who reads this and gains some insight into how her husband and daughter communicate. Maybe it makes another woman think more about her own relationship with her dad. Whatever the case might be, I hope the insights are invaluable.

I hope you get as much from reading this book as I did compiling it. After taking my own notes from these letters, I'm confident that I'll be a better dad to my daughters. I'm confident your relationships will change for the better as well.

Love Unconditionally

I am very much a believer that strong foundations are what make the impossible possible. Loving your daughter unconditionally turns dreams to realities. It unlocks potential. It makes trying new things without fear-of-failure something that your daughter does rather than just thinking about. Loving unconditionally sets the strongest foundation for a unique bond between dad and daughter.

We've always had a special bond. Call it what you will, "I'm the apple that didn't fall far from your tree," "the relationship between father and daughter." When I once complained jokingly to mom that she loved her son more than me…her very straight-faced response, "Well…your father loves you more."

I never questioned the love from either one of you. Now that I have a daughter, I think about the power of love between people and it reminds me of the first thing you ever told me. I know the story well because you tell it at dinner parties, to new parents and to my boyfriends growing up. In the delivery room, when I was born, you say you held me in your arms and whispered, "I will love you unconditionally for the rest of your life and the Red Sox will always break your heart." Everyone laughs and remembers the second part. I remember the first. It has defined our bond. Now that I'm a parent I think about how profound those first words were. And while I'm extremely happy the second part has turned out to be only half-true, I'm especially glad the first hasn't wavered.

The feeling that I was loved unconditionally enabled me to grow up and feel secure, even when things weren't perfect. It allowed me to hear your anger when I did something wrong, take your criticism when I asked for your opinion (even when I didn't ask) and gave me the self-confidence to take risks, seek challenges and admit failure. If you have love; you have something.

You can't underestimate the importance of telling a person you love them unconditionally. You were always so vocal about it. You didn't expect me to know that you loved me just because you were my dad. You made sure I knew that you chose to love me. You told me explicitly that you loved me in every phone call, every evening we said goodnight, at least once a day and after every fight. You wouldn't let me walk away as a child unless I said it too. We even developed our own code for how much we loved each other. "I love you 7," I once said when you asked me just how much I loved you. It is to the moon and back.

You extended this love beyond your children, showing us that you don't need to be born into unconditional. You loved mom instantly and for 40+ years until she died. And you continue to love her now and you don't keep it a secret. You have invited others into this circle and treated them as family. While I have seen people fall from your graces, everyone knows that if they needed you, you would whisper in their ear again.

You have shown me the power this love instills. You have truly loved me unconditionally for my whole life. I am grateful.

It does not mean you treat me like I have no faults. You have always told me that you will be honest with me. I can't say that I always liked this approach you've taken. I much preferred hearing Mom's "If you don't have something nice to say, don't say it all" approach to life. But I do know that it's always easier to hear your Truth because I know there's an unconditional band-aid of love to put on when truth hurts.

I love you 7,
Kate

A Father...

The list is long of reasons I am proud of you and grateful you are my Dad! I have learned so much from you over the years and credit a large part of who I've become, to you. Awh.

You value my opinions – Thanks for always asking me what I thought about a situation…dispelling the 'stereotypes' and teaching me that men and women are true equals.

You set the standard for T R U S T – Being trustworthy and setting an example of how a man should be…how a good man CAN be. A girl should never settle.

You teach intolerance for liars – There's just no excuse for it!! Period.

You instill a deep work ethic – Hard work pays off! And you lead by example.

You challenge my ideologies – You respect my point of view, but constructively, fair and justly, teach me others.

You push me to set goals – To never give up.

You sacrifice – You worked extremely hard, lived modestly and provided for your family on minimal sleep for decades.

...A Friend

You listen without judgment – Through disappointment…you can still offer sound advice.

You are compassionate and friendly – You love to connect with your family and friends. Never would have dreamed I would say this…but, my Dad is a Facebook Junkie! ha

You are genuinely interested in my life and family – You've been an integral part of my son's life and taught him things, given him experiences that I couldn't. Hopefully passing down the characteristics I so deeply adore in you.

You are intelligent, fair and connected – I've nicknamed you the 'walking almanac' – current events, the weather, politics, sports records – you name it, you know it. Jealous.

You display strength – Mental, physical and spiritual – I have never seen you back down from anything you believe in and you stand up for what is right.

You love, unconditionally!

Thanks for everything, from the bottom of my heart!
                                          – *Love, Tweety*

Dear Dad,

I think it's healthy from time to time to reflect on our lives, including our relationships with those closest to us. Since you have been one of the most influential people in my life, I wanted to attempt to articulate what you mean to me and how I feel about our relationship. Anyone who knows you will say you are one of the best people they have ever known. You are kind, generous and unselfish. You are very intelligent and have a great sense of humor. And I am blessed to be one of only two people in the world who gets to call you "Dad."

From the time I was a little girl, you have loved me unconditionally. You accepted me for who I was while challenging me to be the best version of myself. Whether it was encouraging me in my studies, pushing me to ride a roller coaster, or stepping up to coach my sixth grade basketball team (even though I was terrible!), you were always there encouraging me to reach my full potential.

I am grateful to you for SO many things. Of course, you were (and still are!) an amazing provider. I continue to benefit from your financial acumen. Not only have you generously given to me, materially, you are teaching me to fish so I can better understand and manage my own finances. More importantly, however, I appreciate you being such an outstanding role model for me over the years. You are so patient—almost to a fault—and have always played the role of mediator in our family. Growing up, you let me make my own decisions and rarely interfered. However, when you felt strongly about something, you took the initiative to speak up. I distinctly remember a couple of instances in which you felt I was making poor decisions and wrote me letters explaining your position. Because you hardly ever intervened, I definitely took note when you did make your opinions known.

One of your mottos is "work hard, play hard" and you certainly modeled that for us. You have an impressive work ethic. Somehow you managed to work multiple jobs, simultaneously, when we were little; yet, you always had time for us. We took many great family vacations to Florida (I'll never forget cruising the strip in our van in Panama City!) and other fun and educational spots in the US. You bought a house with a swimming pool and let me drive a convertible in high school. You encouraged me in academics and athletics (although, sadly, I didn't get your natural ability!) and helped me become a balanced person. I can't thank you enough for all you have invested in me!

I think we both remember a few key milestones over the years that were very difficult for us as they signified my increasing independence from our core family unit: the day I left for college, the day I left for my new out-of-state job, and the day I got married. Although these events did, indeed, affect the dynamics of our relationship, I feel as close to you now as I ever have. As you remind me on my birthday every year, you dutifully gave me away on my wedding day, but you will never give me away in your heart. And, while I have a few other very special guys in my life now (namely, my husband and two sons), you will always be the first one that had my heart!

I love you, Dad. It brings me great joy to see you as "Pappaw" to my boys. If they grow up to be half the man you are, I will consider myself to have been successful as a mother. THANK YOU for all you have done for me and all you continue to do but, especially, for who you are. I honestly do not think I could have dreamed up a better dad than you. You are definitely one-of-a-kind, and I thank God that you are in my life! I only hope that, as your daughter, I have brought you some happiness and made you proud to be my father. If I have, it is simply a reflection of your influence on my life.

Finally, as you ask me every time we are together, I want to reassure you that we are—and always will be—in the words of Forrest Gump, "just like peas and carrots"!

Love always,
Your daughter, "Ang"

Dear Dad,

I am writing you this letter to let you know how your role in my life has impacted and shaped me. While I found this task to be extremely challenging because there is so much I could say, it really boils down to three items: 1) protection and stability, 2) strong work ethic and 3) love. As a result, I believe myself to be a confident woman with a strong sense of humility. Because our brains are wired the same way, I thought you would appreciate this expression:

My "Dad" Equation

Protection & Stability + Strong Work Ethic + Love = Self-confidence & Humility

---

Protection and Stability—Reflecting on my childhood, I had a strong sense of safety and protection, like you were never going to let anything bad happen to us. You were very strong and capable, and in my young mind, you could fix 'anything' (of course, because you are an engineer!). You always seemed to have an answer for everything which I found amazing and perplexing at times (because how can you really know 'everything' like you said you did?). Somehow, though, I found it very comforting. I continually asked questions and you consistently answered them in a reasonable, logical way. Our connection was very strong and I depended on you greatly as a little girl.

Strong Work Ethic—You have an incredibly strong work ethic which I now come to realize is rare. You came to the United States from Vietnam with literally nothing. You left your home country in your twenties, were immersed in a new culture, had to learn a new language, and had no money. I am in complete awe and humbled by the fact that you were able to raise me and my little brother, as well as support Mom and her parents by bussing tables while pursuing your Engineering degree. I get very emotional thinking about how hard life was for you back then and how scared you must have been. I am now convinced it was your relentless determination that allowed you to persevere through extreme adversity. In your steadfast way, you stayed focused on your goals and were able to provide for your family. You are an excellent role model because of your strong work ethic.

Love—This is probably the most important because without it, the previous two would be difficult, if not impossible, to achieve. Growing up, I didn't know any better but later came to understand that culturally, it was normal for an Asian father to not express outward affection. However, it never bothered me or negatively impacted me because in your strong, quiet way you consistently demonstrated your love for me and our family. Dad, I loved and trusted you and knew you loved me unconditionally.

These three items shaped me significantly—how I interact with my loving husband and my relationship with others; how I can stay laser focused on my goals and know I have the tools and support to get there; how I can challenge myself and not let my fears take over—and doing it with humility and gratitude. I am forever thankful for you, and now see how I can be a strong, loving, positive role model for my children.

I love you, Daddy.

Nhien

What are your thoughts on loving unconditionally?

Be Patient

How can any of us grow if we're not stretched beyond what we're capable of today? Patience is truly a virtue, and as a parent, it's tested. It's downright hard sometimes to be patient with your daughter when your job, others in your family, and other priorities all comingle. Patience is further tested when it's hard to see an end in sight. But the bigger picture tells us to have faith, to be patient, and to recognize the light at the end of the tunnel isn't as far away as we think.

Dear Dad,

When I think about the person I am, you have played an integral part. I have you to thank for many of my qualities: my smile, my somewhat "Type A" personality, my quick wit and quicker temper, my strong will (some might call me stubborn) and most importantly, passion for the people we care about. Some of these are inherited, but I learned a lot along the way from watching you particularly on the importance of family and remembering to enjoy the ride.

I want you to know that I never went a day feeling unloved. Our house was and is a house of huggers—never short of affection, never short of I love you's. There are countless pictures of you and I when I was a baby…you holding me, reading to me, taking me to the park, you name it. I've been told countless times that since the time I was born, I was the apple of your eye. I've heard you tell story after story about my first words, about how I single handedly shut down a few family parties with my crying, and how you would swear off restaurants for good if not enough people came up to you to compliment me. I was your "baby girl," a nickname I still have to this day.

Some of my favorite memories as a kid are with you—family vacations, family get-togethers, playing catch, and our weekly Saturday morning ritual: stopping for donuts, running errands together and going to Grandma's to help her around the house. As she got older, I watched you help her more and more— "a labor of love" you called it. I looked up to you as one of the smartest and most fun people I knew. I had a wonderful childhood with tremendous support from you.

And somehow over time I changed and so did our relationship. As I got a little older and entered my teen years I know that I shunned you. I was a very self-conscious teen and spent most of the time consumed with my image and making sure that whatever I had/did was "cool." Unfortunately by my standards at the time, there was nothing you could do that was right by my eyes and I took my own insecurities out on you. Your same stories were now stupid, your sneeze a bit too loud, and whatever you were wearing was for sure not in style. I know you were just being yourself and hadn't changed from the person you were when I was younger, but suddenly everything in my world felt like it was under a microscope. I know I was bad. Oftentimes, downright mean and hurtful. To call me unpleasant during my teenage years would have been an understatement. Looking back now, I know this came out of my constant concern of what I thought my friends would think when in actuality if I would have just relaxed and not taken things or myself so seriously, I would have been a lot better off. Sometimes you were able to brush me off, other times you yelled back or grounded me. What I do remember is that you always came back with open arms no matter how vicious I got. I don't know how you did it or how you could stand me then, but you did and I won't forget that. I know I apologized from time to time back then (sometimes by my own will, other times not), but looking back I cringe when I think about some of the things I said and am sorry for the time lost.

As an adult, I think our relationship has come a long way from those rough years. College gave me the space I needed to grow up and figure myself out. In recent years you helped me through a particularly rough patch when I was down on myself. You opened up to me and shared your own experiences and the wisdom of hindsight vision. One piece of advice that you gave me I will never forget. During one of these rough patches you reminded me that no one escapes hard times. No one. And to not convince myself that there are people out there that haven't felt this. You reminded me that hard times also mean I have a choice. You told me "You can choose to focus and spend your time and energy on the bad or you can choose to focus and spend your time on what IS working and what IS good. I blinked my eyes and suddenly I am an old man—and the rough times and things I used to worry about when I was your age don't matter now, so why give those things more power and more of your energy than they deserve." I try to keep those words in my back pocket now for when things aren't going my way.

When it comes to our relationship, I know we have had our share of ups and downs. But we have come a long way. I like to think the tougher times have brought us stronger and closer now. I don't always tell you this, but I look up to you as one of the strongest, kindest, and smartest people I know. I'm lucky to call you my dad.

Dad,

You and I have talked a lot over the years, about so many different things. I feel fortunate to say that in our family, I think there's a lot we don't need to tell each other because we all know that we love and support each other as much as any family could, perhaps more. Not many people these days can say that their parents are still happily married after 45 years. I'm grateful to be able to say that mine are, and that I have such an awesome family. Still, sometimes there are things we need to say while we have the chance.

First, I feel like I need to apologize for a couple of things. I don't know why I was afraid when you picked me up when I was little. It was probably because I was afraid you'd turn me upside down (which we all know I was terrified of), but you mentioned once that it hurt your feelings that I cried when you picked me up, and for that I truly apologize. I don't know how many other times I might have done or said things that hurt your feelings. I suppose kids think their parents are immune to such things, especially the spoiled/youngest/only girl types like me who think we can do no wrong. I hope you'll accept this as a blanket apology for any of these instances.

I also feel like I've disappointed you by not living up to my potential and your expectations. I owe you an apology or money or something, for not using my college education to its fullest extent, and for the beautiful wedding that ended in a failed marriage, both of which you so generously paid for. I hope you understand that your generosity is not unappreciated.

You raised my brothers and I to be good people, and my brothers to be fantastic fathers. I recognize how challenging it must have been for you to support us all financially, but I want you to know that in my mind at least, I've never felt like we didn't have enough. We always had everything we needed. I don't know how you did it. I actually feel a sense of pride when comparing childhood vacations and experiences with my friends. I may not have appreciated it at the time, but my childhood was so much fun because of all the different places you took us. While other kids were standing in line at Disney World, we were watching the Space Shuttle take off and wandering around at Gatorland Zoo. Instead of going to Virginia Beach, we were somewhere in Texas looking at dinosaur footprints in a river. You broadened our horizons, educated us by doing all the things you wanted to do. Our travels and conversations while I was in high school especially, after my brothers had left home and it was just you and I going places together, will always remain some of my most cherished memories. I can't think of a better way to spend a summer than going someplace a little different, or participating in a hobby that's a little different but that introduces a person to an entirely new family and so many different places and things.

You probably don't realize, as a shy and humble person, the influence you have on everyone around you. People who know you admire you for living wholly and without excuses or complaints in spite of the challenges you have faced in your life. Your sense of humor and quirky personality have made you beloved to so many people—your friends, family, students, and community. You are, without a doubt, the most intelligent person I have ever met. It amazes me the way you retain everything you read and have the patience and ability to explain pretty much anything to anyone. As similar as we are, I wish I could be more like you.

This letter can never, ever tell you all the reasons I admire, respect, and love you, but I hope you get the idea. And another thing (because I know reading that just made you smile)! Once, when we were at the Ohio Brew Week, you thanked me for going with you because all of your friends had deserted you. "Not that you're not my friend, but you know what I mean," you said. I want you to know that words cannot express how proud I am to be your daughter, and also to call you my friend.

K

What You Are

©1992 Randy Weeks

See the little girl smiling with me
Picture taken when she was just three
In the days when she said she was gonna marry Daddy
Now the little boys call on my phone
My little girl's got this mind of her own
Sometimes seems that her growing up is
Easier on her than me

But what you are is all right with me
Dads & daughters they disagree, sometimes
Now you think I'm old fashioned
Believe me through the years we'll be friends
'Cause what you are is a delight to me
A gift of God & a mystery
I swear
No matter what you do
No power on earth can change
My love for you

Little girl in the grown-up disguise
There'll be times when, with tears in your eyes
You will ask my advice
And still never think twice
About not taking it
Some decisions you make will be wrong
It'll break my heart
Many times before you're grown
We'll have laughter & fights
It's all part of this life
Someday I'll let you go
But everyday I'll be there

'Cause what you are is all right with me
Dads & daughters they disagree, sometimes
Now you think I'm old fashioned
Believe me through the years we'll be friends
And what you are is a delight to me
A gift of God & a mystery
I swear
No matter what you do
No power on earth can change
My love for you

Dad,

As I read over those lyrics to the song you wrote me when I was just 13 years old, I again understand that I would not be the woman I am today without the love and guidance you gave to my life. I look back and realize what a handful I was, a "little girl in the grown up disguise"—this smart mouthed teenager who was rebellious and boy crazy. I can't imagine how many nights you laid awake worrying about me and the decisions I was making. I wonder how you were still able to gently guide me along the right path without judgment or yelling, but you did. By the time you and Mom divorced, when I was 17, you had become my best friend. You were the one I called late at night from my college dorm when some boy broke my heart. No matter what time of night that phone rang, you always picked up and gave me your expert advice—even though you knew I'd "never think twice about not taking it." Whether I took your advice or not, just hearing your voice made things make more sense.

It must have been so difficult for you to figure out how to handle the situations and life I was living —the nights I didn't come home, the countless loser boyfriends, my less than stellar group of friends. I laugh when I think about the fact that you were the first person I told when I thought I was pregnant at only 18 years old. Usually a dad would be the LAST person a teenage girl would tell, but I was scared and the only person I felt I could really trust was you. I so very much apologize for being so out of control back then and I'll always be grateful that you were able to handle those situations and be there for me. You always encouraged me to have open lines of communication with you. I'm not sure you realized what kind of conversations you signed up for with your wild and severely headstrong daughter.

You definitely weren't a pushover and I appreciate that. You always had this uncanny ability to be able to put me in my place without making me feel like a bad person. You helped me make the most important decisions in my life by making me think for myself. That was a gift that has surely helped me succeed in life, especially when I made the scary move from Ohio to New York City all by myself. I remember very fondly the drive from Cincinnati to Cleveland where my flight to New York was departing. We talked about life and love and everything in between on that 3 hour drive. I was terrified of the life ahead of me and of leaving everything I loved and knew to chase this career in the big city. That talk, like so many others, was invaluable. At 23, I was finally old enough to really listen and understand the advice you were giving me instead of just letting it go in one ear and out the other. You told me to believe in myself, believe in what got me to where I was at that point in my life and to take in and appreciate every single moment. I miss you every day since I made that move away from home more than 8 years ago, but I know that it was one of the best decisions of my life and I couldn't have done it without you.

The late night phone calls about heartbreak and life's battles have diminished since I met my husband Steve and I believe that without a male role model in my life like you, I would've never found a man like him. A man so similar to you in demeanor, both peaceful and strong and able to make me laugh until I almost pee my pants. I have Steve now but no one can ever replace my daddy. Dancing with you at my wedding to the song you wrote for me all those years ago will always be one of the most cherished moments of my life. Now that I am the age where I am ready to start my own family, I hope that Steve and I will handle parenting with the grace and understanding that you did. You will still be one of the first people I call when life hands me something I don't think I can handle. And I know that even though "the little girl in a grown up disguise" is a grown woman now, you will continue to guide me and help me through tough times just as you always have. No power on earth can change my love for you.

What are your thoughts on being patient?

Be Mindful

Being your daughter's dad is an art, not a science. With no manual, we test some things, see if they work, and then try again. Sometimes we work so hard over *here*…that we forget about what's over *there*. Sometimes it's by choice, and sometimes by accident. But in either case, as a dad, it's our job to be mindful of our actions and the consequences that can come from them.

Dad,

As I thought about our relationship at this stage of my life, and what your role as my dad truly means to me, I wanted you to know a few things.

It's funny, but reflecting on our relationship it's clear to me that when I was younger I was actually kind of scared of you. Don't get me wrong, I always knew you loved me and would take care of me the best you could, giving me access to every opportunity within your control. Maybe it had something to do with the business suit you wore or the briefcase you carried…but you seemed pretty intimidating and unapproachable. Maybe that's why I never really got in trouble. I don't think I can really remember getting yelled at or being spanked for misbehaving by you or Mom. Ever since I was little I feared messing up or not being "good" because it would disappoint you. So I got straight A's, I played every sport, volunteered, sang in choir, played the piano, went to church and participated in any club that would let me. And regardless of how well I did you pushed harder. Do you remember when in high school you had me read a book on Re-engineering and report on it over dinner? Now, I did get into a great college and landed a job at a great company and I know you had a lot to do with these successes.

But, I think it was all at a cost. I feared failing. Maybe that doesn't seem like a bad thing, but I believe it profoundly impacted my life, and still does. Sometimes the fear showcases itself in weird unimportant ways. Believe it or not, I hate going to new group fitness classes at the gym because I don't want to seem like I don't know what to do or because I'm nervous I'll look like a wimp compared to everyone else. That's kind of silly, but it's the truth. But this fear of not "being good" has pushed its way into other parts of my life. Looking back on my college years and young adult life I realize that I actually held back from having fun! I would always be the first to leave a party and when I got home I often asked myself why. I think I convinced myself it was because I wanted to get a good night's sleep so I could have a productive weekend. Wow—that's pretty horrible for a 22 year old to say. I missed out on so many opportunities to enjoy life and make memories with my friends. That said, I think there was something bigger. Unlike most of my friends, I never really had boyfriends. Ever. In fact the only relationship to last more than 3 months is the one that I'm in now—and he is the man I am engaged to marry. The idea of a boyfriend made me nervous. In high school I remember going to the Friday night hockey games and being queasy because I might see the boy I had a crush on. Not butterflies…pure nausea. And in college when the guy I had liked for years was finally interested in me I made a beeline for the door. Just like I was afraid of disappointing you, I was scared I would disappoint them. What's sad is that it took me 30 years to get over it and begin to have healthy relationships.

I bet you never would have guessed that your fathering would impact my life the way it has. You also probably don't realize how much you've influenced my life and behavior for the better either. I've learned how to express gratitude and show thoughtfulness through hand-written notes, just like your mom taught you. I use data and logic before emotion to guide my decisions. I'm reserved and only talk when I have something to say. I'm stubborn, but in a good way :) I am generous with my time and money for a good cause—whatever that may be. I try to surprise others with little gifts to let them know I care or celebrate a success. I am strong, hard-working, independent and willing to challenge things that I don't agree with. And while you struggle with the fact that I am not a practicing Catholic, I am a good Christian, just like you.

There is so much you in me—Mom says so all the time. Your love and support have been unwavering. And when I have children—God-willing—I hope they feel the love and support that I learned from you. While perhaps our relationship wasn't perfect, it was pretty good. And it got exceedingly better when I finally learned to replace fear of you with respect for you. Dad, I love you.

Dear Dad,

We have been through some good times, and some pretty crappy times through the years. And, I don't think I ever have expressed to you how some of those times have made an impact on my life.

I know that whatever doesn't kill me makes me stronger.

I know that I CAN do things on my own.

I know that you trust me.

I know a lot more about boat & car engines than an average woman.

I can handle a riding lawn mower, snowmobile, and go cart like a champ.

I think I can honestly find many good ways I have been affected by losing mom, and having to deal with our struggles with it, and you becoming a single parent, etc. But, since I have had Evan, the pain felt from the way you handled 'life' after mom died seems to cut deeper than ever before.

You were not the only one struggling. We were all struggling to deal with life during those years. I chose to bury my head in sports and school, and you took a more 'liquid' approach and found vodka as a way to dull the pain. Travis and Christopher were also struggling, and in many different ways than you or I.

I can't deny that you had your plate full. And, looking back I can see times where you were doing your best to be our Dad. But those seem to be overshadowed by times when you chose to ignore being Dad (and those times were usually pretty important). I will admit that I may not have made it easy at times. But I was a child, trying to grow, and learn, and make sense of the world in a world that made no sense.

Whether or not people realize it, everyone leads by example. And, even if they lead by bad example, the person behind has to decide how to make the most of it. It wasn't pretty walking behind you, but at least I was able to learn from it, learn to understand it, and learn to appreciate all that it gave me. I like to think that Mom was also walking along side me.

We have made much progress in our relationship in recent years. Having you in my life is good.

I forgave you. I thank you. I love you.

—*Suzanne W*

Hi Daddy,

I know I don't always tell you how wonderful of a father you've been but hopefully you get that from the little things I try to do to make sure you know I love you. You have done an amazing job of not just being a father but fathering a daughter. You are more than merely the person who paid my tuition or reminded me that I "didn't need that chump anyway" whenever one of my relationships ended. You are the man who set the standard for what I would accept from the men in my life and for that I am eternally grateful. I always knew our relationship was special but it wasn't until I became a young woman, seriously dealing with men and establishing boundaries for how they would deal with me, that I really understood the magnitude of your importance in my life and in the development of my character.

I remember the point when I realized how important having grown up with my father as the man in my life was. It was around the time I was applying to business school and I had become really good friends with some really outstanding young women. From the looks of it, we were all cut from the same cloth—bright, young, attractive (if I may say so myself :) and headed into graduate programs at some of the country's most prestigious institutions…Harvard, Northwestern, Duke…you name it. As time went by and we became closer friends I learned more about them and saw how they interacted with men and more importantly, how their interactions were affected by men. We were all looking for the same thing—someone to love us, someone to settle down with, and someone to call our own. The variable that became strikingly evident was what I called the "father factor."

I began to realize that, while we all had our issues with the guys we dated, no one ever disrespected me or treated me as badly as they often treated my friends. This was because, as a result of my relationship with you, I knew the minimums a man needed to deliver and recognized when they weren't being met. I always considered "if a man can't do more for me than my daddy does then why put up with him." So, when he wasn't treating me like a lady I was okay saying "when." This alone made my twenties much easier and less dramatic.

But Daddy, I have to tell you something. While you were an amazing father, you were a terrible husband and witnessing your disregard for my mother, your wife, has had an effect on me as well. As I have become older and am now considering marriage, I realize that

I have subconsciously developed this overwhelming flight response when situations with the man I love are not ideal. It's not because I don't want to be his wife but because I don't want to turn out like you— unfulfilled in my marriage but too afraid to be on my own to leave. People often say that women marry men like their fathers. I hope that's true. What scares me to death is that the man I marry will be less like my father and more like my mothers' husband. I know it seems contradictory to feel this way and I don't know how to explain it much better than I have. On the one hand, because of you I have standards and boundaries. On the other hand, I lack patience and resolve.

So what do you do with this? Honestly, I just wanted you to know how your influence and your role in my decision making processes has evolved in a way I had not imagined. I don't love you any less or think any less of you. It's just interesting to understand the many different ways you have impacted my life. You are one man with many roles and I truly have always felt how important your role as a father is to you. I guess the real shocker is that I now also feel how unimportant your role of a husband may have been as well. Just something to think about.

I love you.

What are your thoughts on being mindful?

Be Amazing

A dad is human. A dad is a person. You're not just a dad. You have interests & hobbies, likes & dislikes. Some of those revolve around your daughter, and some of those were formed long before she came along. These letters tell the stories of dads who played what is sometimes the hardest role to play as a dad—themselves. What came from that was…well, amazing.

DAD,

It's amazing when you grow up and you realize your parents are actually real people; complete with their own fears, flaws, and fancies. When I was old enough to realize this, I was also lucky enough to discover that my dad was really pretty amazing. For most of my childhood, you made it look so easy. When I realized there was actually a person behind my dad, one who had to go to work every day, come home, do some home improvement project, knock out some math homework with me and still manage a smile and a good dinner time story—it made it even more special.

You always taught me through your own actions that it was OK to cry, and boy did you cry. You taught me it was OK to be strange, to be weird, and to be myself; which was conveniently easy for me since those two were one in the same. You also taught me to pay attention to and be amazed by the little things in life. And this, I think, is the thing I am most proud that I got from you (not to mention your super skinny ankles, rutty red cheeks, and extreme lack of flexibility).

You taught me to make connections between little things in the world, between science and math, how these things shaped the history of our world and 'how cool' is it that it all fits together? Making these connections and seeing the bigger picture meant I was continuously amazed by things in the world around me and never took things for granted, always understanding the reason or 'why' behind something. As cheesy as it may sound, this is the type of teaching that keeps young girls moving in a positive direction vs. the direction of many of my peers. This is the type of teaching that keeps you interested in learning more, wanting to enrich yourself with knowledge, no matter how trivial it seems, because it's all part of the bigger picture.

I know now that it wasn't easy to do this. You first had to take the time to be patient, not dumping all these amazing little facts on me at once, but slowly fostering my interest. Through stories at the dinner table, lessons in the car on the way to soccer practice, a 'fun fact' pointed out here and there— always patient, always teaching. Secondly, you had to not get discouraged. Yes, at times we all prefer being lazy teenagers over most anything else in the world, however you found 'teaching opportunities' in pretty much every situation. You kept it corny, you knew your limits, but you always sought to reach out and make some sort of connection. Lastly, you showed me that I should be proud of what I know and to never let being a 'nerd' be referred to as a bad thing. I never grew up with the notion that it wasn't a girl's place to be smart, or sporty, or tough, or any one of those things because I was just following the example that being me was whatever I wanted it to be.

And yes, I'm so happy I decided to come live with you.

Love,

The Kid

Dear Dad,

I've compiled a list of things I want to thank you for because those things have influenced the direction of my life in some way (although admittedly, sometimes not in the direction you wanted them to go :)

Thank you for the quirky, unforgettable songs that can soothe any child. The "Daisy and Ginger" song, dedicated to the best Beagle puppies a girl could ever have, is still engrained in my memory. (I'm humming it right now). It was the perfect song for bedtime and I hear that it even put your newest grandbaby to sleep just last week.

Thank you for the impromptu dance sessions in

the kitchen. They helped prepare me for the stage later in life. And while I'm sure you'd love if I was a prima ballerina, being a professional belly dancer is just as good, right?

Thank you for introducing me to awesome music in my younger years. Jimi Hendrix's "Band of Gypsies" is a much better way to kickoff the Christmas morning gift opening frenzy than traditional Christmas songs.

(Although just be sure you don't lose your edge on that one...it was Mom who asked for Metallica tickets for Mother's Day!)

Thank you for the life advice. I vividly remember you telling me as a teenager "don't get pregnant and don't get arrested." Success! No grandbabies or arrests, although now that I'm 30, married and refusing to have kids, you're probably eating those words on that 'don't get pregnant' part. I'm just doing what you told me!

Thank you for the driving advice. Anyone who drives with me knows the "Katy's Dad School of Driving" tips. To name a few: Check your mirrors every 5–10 seconds, always roll with the flow of traffic, don't speed, and never turn right into the middle lane! Admittedly your backseat was sometimes annoying, but I guess you don't get to millions of miles of safe driving without knowing a thing or 2 about how to drive.

Thank you for being a hippie at heart. You are a legend with my high school friends for letting me go to Woodstock '99, even after Mom said no (sorry Mom...you have to be the mean parent for this part).

I still remember you waking me up on the morning tickets went on sale (Mom wasn't home) and driving me to the Thriftway Ticketmaster hub saying "I didn't get to go to Woodstock and I can't let that happen to you."

Thank you for having a weird-ass sense of humor. The hours we spent watching "Ren and Stimpy" have definitely influenced my own sense of humor. And while I know raising a teenage daughter was tough, at least I could make you laugh by singing Stimpy's favorite tune: "La lalala hmm hmm. Happy happy hmm hmm."

Thank you for my exposure to the outdoors. I vividly remember camping out at various sites across Ohio, boating at Lake Cumberland, and hiking at Buzzard's Roost (or being carried at Buzzard's Roost when I didn't want to hike). While some of those trips ended with 1000s  of bug bites covering my entire body or dirty fishing hooks embedded underneath my skin, I still learned to savor and appreciate being outside in nature.

Speaking of Lake Cumberland, thank you for the advice on how to survive it. My friends and I always review the "Katy's Dad" checklist of lake rules (even though we're now all 30+ years of age!):

1) Don't get in the golf cart with anyone going down the hill.

2) Don't get on a boat with anyone who appears to be drinking.

3) If you get bit by a poisonous snake, kill it and take it with you to the hospital.

Check. Check. Check. (wait...except on that last one about the snake...are you serious???)

So to sum all this up, all I can really say is "thank you Daddy." I wouldn't be where I am without you.

Love,
Your Angel

In these last couple years, as I've started to consider myself an actual adult, I find myself thinking a lot about how I was brought up, your style as a father, and you as a person. Is all of it perfect? No. But I wouldn't trade it for anything.

Thank you for having the patience to comb out my long wet hair when I was too young to manage it and just couldn't bare Mom's, um, *aggressive* touch. I think she was the only one bothered by the fact that you never really got the tangles underneath.

Thanks for teaching me how to bait a hook. I don't remember the last time I did it and I'm not sure when I ever will again, but at least I know how. Mom tells the story about how nervous she was that her little girl was handling sharp things while you were so patient and trusting that I would follow your instructions. What a perfect analogy for the rest of my childhood and adolescence!

I don't think you ever really spoiled me too much that I can remember, but I will say that there's no better breakfast than half a grapefruit that you've sectioned perfectly, waiting for me in the refrigerator. Ask how often I eat grapefruit now. I'm too lazy.

Depending on the year and my age, I was either

excited or annoyed by the fact that you always insisted Sissy and I wear dresses for Easter and Christmas. "Little girls should wear nice dresses." Old fashioned and impractical as it seemed, hunting for eggs in white tights and white patent leather shoes, and mud. Slipping along Grandma's driveway in the snow and cold in white tights and black patent leather shoes. It's stayed with me—now I find myself teetering along in heels and pencil skirts. It's a *holiday*. You're supposed to dress nice.

Your final words on fashion are probably "Hey, be a trend setter." The response to complaints of not having Guess Jeans and the latest fashions. Yet, your fondness for vintage cool, or maybe it's just your refusal to get rid of anything, brings to mind the year you wore an old green corduroy suit to the family Christmas Eve party. Mom was mortified and I was in awe. It was probably 1995 or so and grunge was god. Corduroy was everywhere. You weren't trying to be hip or ironic. You were just dressing nice for the holiday. I got over not having stylish clothes, but I'll never get over that green suit. Badass.

Your most iconic outfit has got to be your greasy blue work uniform. I'd look for that uniform from the stage at every dance recital. I'm ashamed to remember that your uniform embarrassed me sometimes. Now I think about it and smile, because it means that you rushed straight from work to be there. Every year. I think about it with pride, because if you weren't in that uniform, I wouldn't have been in dance lessons.

Thanks for taking me out into the woods every year to pick a cedar tree for Christmas. I was too young to understand why our tree never looked like the $50 trees that other people had, but it didn't matter. All five of us decorated it together, but I got to put the Christmas Spirit on the top. I loved those mornings in the woods. But I don't miss the bagworms on the cedar trees.

I think about the time you told me that Bob Dylan was a poet and how, for the first time in quite awhile, I felt like you and I had something in common. I don't think anyone who truly listens to "Lay Down Your Weary Tune" can disagree.

This fondness for classic rock combined with enough afternoons spent at car shows and countless evenings spent at the drag strip gave me just enough knowledge to be able to talk to boys about something they found interesting. I think some of them would have rather hung out in the garage with you than take me to the movies, but to this day, any guy who spent any time at our house always asks about you. Then he immediately recounts how impressed he was that any time we left the house, after Mom's warnings to be careful, be home on time, and call if we were going anywhere else, your final words for the night were always "Be cool."

You trusted that you and Mom had done your job, that I knew how to act once I left the house, that I was smart enough to make good choices. I was certainly no angel, but there were plenty of moments when I'd consider you telling me "If something doesn't feel right, it's probably not" and go from there. I think it worked all right. You must have too, when you and I had a talk about whether I should go away for college or not, and you told me that it was important for everyone to spend some time away from home. I needed that.

Even though I've been away from home for a long time, the first warm spring day makes me want to ride on the back of your Norton. I think about summer nights on the back porch, listening to the Reds while you pet your bird dog and chew tobacco. Sometimes when I wash my face at the end of the day, I wish that you were in the next room playing guitar along with some Stones or Beatles song, like you were so many nights when I was younger.

Thank you. For being you. For the parenting decisions you and Mom made, for the imagination I developed as a result of what we couldn't afford, for the times our family spent together because we had nowhere else to go and no money to do anything. For everything. I think most of the memories and experiences that shaped our relationship were things you'd have done regardless, that you didn't even realize you were doing, that you still do now. And that's cool.

Love,
Your Bambina
Robyn H.

Dad,

How can I begin to put into words the profound effect you have had on my life? You have taught me so many lessons, and I now hope to pass them on to my children. You provided me with a wonderful childhood that was filled with its ups and downs. I have such fantastic memories from growing up and none of them would be possible without you.

I remember when I was really little and Mom was still working on Saturday morning. You were in charge of breakfast, and I can still smell the burnt blueberry waffles from the toaster. Then I got to watch the Smurfs. I loved those little blue creatures. Then you got to pick a show. There were quite a few Saturday mornings when I remember watching the WWF or whatever the new acronym for it is now.

Another one of my favorite memories is our movie weekends. I am sure Mom just wanted some quiet time, but you and I got to go to the movies. Mind you that some of the movie choices were questionable (who takes a five year old to see Die Hard?), but it didn't matter. Just you and me and a bowl of popcorn, but only halfway through the movie, I loved those weekend afternoons.

We both know that sometimes life can lead to

places you never wanted to go. The summer I was sick is one of those times. They may not be the most pleasant memories, but I will never forget how you took care of me that summer. After a day at work, you would meet Mom for dinner and then you got the night shift. Now, I am sure no shift was pleasant, but the night shift was hard, because I was so sick. You never lost your temper, you just cleaned me up and told me to go back to bed. I also remember the afternoon when we had to shave my head. I am sure that this was not an easy task, but I don't remember you being outwardly upset. Your brave face made me put on one as well.

Then you became coach. No matter what sport I was playing you were there on the sidelines. I will never forget my first varsity basketball game. The referee had made a questionable call. There was some murmuring among the crowd when out of nowhere I heard: "Open your eyes fat boy!" Even though it was pretty embarrassing, it was nice to know that you were at the game cheering us on.

I have looked up to you as long as I can remember. The way which you devoted yourself to our family has influenced me profoundly. I cannot remember an event that you were not present for. Of course you were there for all of the birthdays and graduations, but you also made it a point to be at my sporting events and award presentations. This made me feel so special; because there were many other girls I know that did not have a dad who was willing or able to devote that amount of time to their family.

Thank you for always being there for me and being involved in my life. Thank you for providing me great memories despite the not so great circumstances that life sometimes puts in your path. As I have grown up and moved on, I am glad that our relationship has also evolved. I love the fact that I can call my dad one of my best friends.

With love and gratitude always.

What are your thoughts on being amazing?

Be *The* Example

Hundreds of books have argued over what the exact traits are of great leaders. Parents are the leaders of their family, and what has shown to be true through countless generations of these leaders is that setting the right example is critically important. Walking the talk, living your ideals, and recognizing that actions speak louder than words are sure-fire ways for you to have a profound influence on your daughter.

Dad,

As you approach 70, I thought it would be a fitting time to share with you the tremendous impact you have had on my life and on the lives of my children. There are three areas where you have most influenced me and shaped me into the woman I am: your steadfastness, your continual passion for learning, and your infectious love of life and I will be eternally grateful.

Ever since I can remember, you have been steadfast. You seem to be the rock that everyone relies on: friends, family, neighbors, and anyone who needs a hand. You seem to outstretch yours without expecting anything in return, even when it comes to money. Yet, steadfastness is a greater value than money—it is fellowship and a trust between others that money cannot buy at any price. It is being even-keeled, honest, patient, kind, and having a presence. All these qualities are so invaluable I am not sure anyone will ever be able to quantify your contributions to their lives.

Your contributions to life have been fueled by your continual passion for learning. I can't recall a time that you weren't trying to figure out how something worked, reading the newspaper religiously on a daily basis, and soaking up all the world has to offer like a sponge. Both of my children have inherited this trait—

both by nature and nurture, and I am so privileged that you are around to help those passions cross over generational lines.

Generational lines are something that are blurry in your eyes. Your infectious love of life has kept you far younger than your almost 70 years—in spirit and in wit. You are funny, energetic, in touch and willing to try new things—constantly taking a ride on this wild rollercoaster we call life. You have no sense of fear. I see the zeal for living in you when you play with my children, when you cook dinner, and when you hike the hills of your boyhood home in Kentucky. Always breathing in the air of experience in order to make life memories for those around you.

I know in recent months you have not been in good health and it worries me. What will come of us if you are not around? I pray with my children on a daily basis for your longevity. The outpouring of love and support you have given to our family over the years is immeasurable and I am proud to call you my father and my best friend. There are not enough days in life to celebrate your contributions. So, I simply want to say thank you. Thank you for the example that you set for me to follow and in turn for my children to follow.

May all daughters who have fathers be as fortunate as I have been to have you in my life. You have given me a peace of heart, a calmness of mind, and a happiness of soul in this life that I can only hope I pass on to my children. I love you dad.

Dad,

Having been on the go constantly for the past several months, I've been reflecting a lot lately about how I may create better balance in my life. Through this process, I find myself frequently coming back to you and the invaluable lessons you've taught me over the years. From as far back as I can remember, whenever I was feeling excited, confused, elated or anxious you would be among the first I'd phone to share my thoughts. You would consistently offer words of encouragement while also providing realistic feedback and asking questions about what I would do to either relish the moment or get in better control of a situation. Over and above this, you shared with me your incredible sense of self-awareness. Without you, I'd have not been as well-off in understanding what it truly takes to not only recognize stimuli but also resolutions in extremely stressful times. Even when I was a complete terror in high school (like when I was really mad and decided to punch a hole in my bedroom wall, or when I would find myself mediating petty arguments among my friends), you were the one to come in to my room after and talk it out with me. You understood that there had to be a rational root to the angst and were willing to do everything in your power to help me come up with ways to better release and resolve in any scenario. You were always able to bring my thought process back to reality and through that exercise teach me to better understand how powers of the mind manifest physically. I remember when I would study with you at the dining room table, many times you'd physically have to open my hands as I'd not realized they were fully clenched for hours as I was studying for my calculus exams. I took these lessons with me through college where you were not as close by, and further into business school, relationships and career.

Beyond your working with me to become better in control, you were (and still are) one who practices what he preaches. It's often times I've met folks who claim to operate a certain way in life, but are actually failures when it comes to execution. Understanding it's not always been easy for you either, I've never seen you as 'all talk, no action.' It's a truly remarkable way to be and I hope I'm able to emulate you—certainly trying. I know I've made major strides, but still have much to grow. In addition to being able to now recognize certain behaviors in myself, this knowledge has really helped me to relate to my friends and colleagues and work with them through stressful periods. I'm always hearing from people that not only am I super self-aware, but also extremely patient and not critical. I'm able to (because of your example) provide a sense of calm and positivity. This is a strength I undoubtedly learned from being so close to you, Dad. I am sure that growing up, I was the least patient and most critical one in our immediate family. Again, I'm still working on this—no one's perfect, but at least I can use this power for good with others and hope that someday I'll find the balance within myself too.

With that, wanted again to say 'Thank You' for supporting me in everything I do, vocalizing your pride, being honest in your evaluation and teaching me from your experience. I am so lucky to have you as a father and role model. Love you.

Dad,

Since I've never really told you what you've done for me as a dad, I'm writing this letter now to let you know how I feel.

First of all, you've influenced me probably more than anyone else in my life. Starting from my childhood, I think you were the most encouraging of anything I wanted to do. Maybe it was learning to ride a bike, or learning to swim, or play tennis, or play the violin, or be an actress. You were my biggest cheerleader. It's because of this that today I take on so many challenges. I try things all the time that scare me to death, but I face them because you taught me at a young age that I could achieve anything. Not enough girls are told yes, and I was always told I could do it, whatever it was.

Weekly ski trips to Paoli Peaks, camping, long bike rides, tennis…you spent most of your free time with me. You could have taken that time off to relax, but instead you took me somewhere to do something fun, and to teach me something. And to make me appreciate the simple pleasures in life.

Your love for acting has clearly rubbed off on me. I know that I technically started acting first, but I think your enthusiasm when I asked you to play pretend games with me encouraged me to pursue acting. You always played along. When I wrote Santa notes, you wrote back. When I performed my magic shows in our family room, you bought a ticket from me and pretended to be wowed by my tricks. Even though you probably wanted me to do something practical, you took me to see plays (remember when you snuck me into a sold out performance because you really wanted me to see that play?) and came to every one of my performances multiple times. Your encouragement gave me permission to do what I loved.

You've also taught by example. Hard work, strong morals, a good sense of ethics. This I've learned from watching you. You have a career in something you believe in, which taught me to never settle for less. You stand strongly by your morals, and have taught me to do the same. (and thankfully you've passed on your political beliefs to me, too, but I won't get political here…)

I do, however, often fear that I disappoint you. You've set such high standards for yourself and I hope I haven't let you down. I know you're proud of me, but I also know that you have high hopes for me and sometimes I worry I don't meet that.

That said, I know you're proud of me, and that you're always supporting me and cheering me on along the way. I hope you understand how much you have done for me, and how grateful I am. Even if I sometimes go for weeks without talking to you, I feel this gratitude everyday.

Love,
Alice

Dad—

As I thought about our relationship at this stage of my life, and what your role as my dad truly means to me, I wanted you to know a few things. I know I have tried with countless Hallmark cards to tell you how I feel, but none seems to truly encompass everything that you mean to me…but I sure have bought my fair share to try. :)

Growing up, I quickly learned from you the core values that are inherent in my daily interactions, just by looking up to you. I learned to be loyal to those you care about, be true to your word, to maintain and follow-through on your commitments. I watched as you were a role model for hard work, and to be generous with everything you can give. I always saw you as successful in everything you did, and because of that have set high standards for myself—not only to try and make you proud, but also to strive to be like you.

You have always been my protector, my advisor, and my silent supporter. You allowed me to learn on my own, but never let me make too many mistakes or get hurt beyond recovery. You gave me advice mostly when asked, and provided me a balanced way of looking at the world before making any decisions or actions. I see now how family, friends, legal advisees seek your counsel—and know how lucky I am to have grown up with such wise advice and insightful perspective, and count on it still.

You challenged me to try new things, and especially remember your support and personal coaching when I learned to ride my bike, ski, ice skate, and play softball —for which I say I was a "jack of all trades" as a kid, and now have an inherent curiosity to see the world and try everything once. You encouraged me to reach high and pursue anything I wanted, and believe that in each of those moments I had confidence to do that knowing you (and Mom) had faith in me.

What I realize now as an adult are the tough choices you must have made, and sacrifices necessary to be able to live the life we have. You had to make career decisions to meet the family needs, missed social engagements for scheduled obligations, and dedicated time to others when you didn't have minutes to spare. You did this quietly without notice, and looking back I learned that is where I learned about strength—which is the most dominant quality that you have displayed recently—and am more inspired by you now than ever before… You and Mom have endured much, but have tons to be proud of, as our family of six is rich in life and love for each other—and have strong relationships with relatives that are held together through your example.

I remember the moments growing up when our family truly embraced and enjoyed life—road trip vacations, dressing up at Halloween, playing outside in the neighborhood. You also have a story for everything—whether it is for entertainment (including laughing at your own jokes), or for some life lesson example. I use both of these aspects as my inspiration not to take things in life too seriously.

I'm thrilled that at this stage in life you are starting to be able to enjoy the finer things—and even more value that we can do it together. From lovely meals together as a family, trying a new glass of wine, attending crazy sporting events or theater shows, or just watching TV—those moments together are some of the best of my life, and I value them more than I could have ever imagined as a child. My wish for you is that you can now "play" as hard as you have "worked" for all of these years—and that you know how special you are to me and truly loved and admired.

Love—MLS

What are your thoughts on being the example?

Be There and Be Accountable

Themes that naturally arose from these letters—unconditional love, patience, being amazing, and setting the right example—are all challenging enough for a dad. They're even harder to do when Dad isn't around.

Dear Dad,

Growing up, I idolized you. You were so different than other dads—you were young, fun, and so funny. I craved your attention. I would do everything that you would do, including wearing Carhartt and watching NASCAR (and thinking it was a real sport). We shared a love of cats and Dirty Harry movies. I embraced our Georgia roots. I would make the 12 hour car ride with you to visit Granny even when mom and Jess wouldn't. I always wanted your approval.

Even though we had fun when I was growing up, we weren't close. I didn't go to you for advice. That was mom's job. This was exacerbated by the fact that you weren't home enough. When you took the sales job that required you to travel all over the Midwest, you were only home on the weekends. And when you were home, you would sleep. All day. I understand now that you were clinically depressed and you and mom were in a bad marriage, but you hid that from us. All I knew was that my dad wasn't really around.

When I was a senior and Jess was a sophomore in college, you moved out and to a sketchy part of town near the airport. That's when the verbal assault on mom began. You blamed her for EVERYTHING that had gone wrong in your life and in our lives. You cried to me on the phone. I got ulcers worrying about you, when I was supposed to be working on my senior design project. Mom was not blameless in the situation, but she never badmouthed you. Eight months later, you moved 1,000 miles away, on a whim. You said it was because the rent was the lowest in the country, but we all knew better; you moved there for a woman. Turns out she's a nice woman and she loves you, but what kind of woman gets into a relationship with a married man and convinces him to move 1,000 miles away from his children? I lost a lot of respect for you then.

Since you moved away, I have seen you once a year. You act as if you know me, but you don't. Our conversations are relegated to the weather. And your job. You don't ask me about my job or my life or what my dreams are or fears are. You keep a distance. I don't know if you see too much of mom in me or if you never wanted children in the first place. I feel indifferent about you. I love you because you're my dad, but we don't have much in common, and I don't want to waste my energy trying to establish a real relationship with you. After the divorce, I used to defend you to Jess. I blamed your abusive upbringing. But there comes a point when you have to take accountability for your actions. I no longer defend you; I say you are who you are and you probably won't change.

To this day, you can't let anything go. You still blame mom for pushing you away. But you have NEVER taken responsibility for being an absent parent. You should have some respect for the mother of your children, but you do not. Even though you are happily married to someone else and have been divorced for 8 years, you can't let go. You aren't man enough to be a good father; you are too selfish. The first male relationship that a woman has is with her father. This relationship will stay with her throughout her life and will affect all future relationships she has with men. I have achieved a great relationship in spite of you. The man I chose to be my husband will be an excellent father. He is all the things that you are not: engaged, caring, devoted, loving, and honest. He isn't perfect, but he's willing to admit when he's wrong and when he doesn't know what to do. I think we'll be a good team.

Dad, I miss the carefree days of my early childhood, when you loved mom and before the lying and cheating started. I wish that you could make it up to Jess and me somehow. I wish you wanted to make it up to us. I look forward to the future with my family, and I hope you'll make an effort to be part of it.

Dad,

As I thought about our relationship at this stage of my life, and what your role as my dad truly means to me, I wanted you to know a few things.

I would say that in most cases where a dad is an absent figure there is some animosity towards that father. It's funny because with you, I feel no animosity, only thanks.

I want you to know that I appreciate you keeping your distance throughout my life, I appreciate you not providing us with any help and support as we grew up, and I appreciate knowing that substance abuse drove you to separate yourself from our family.

All of these things, the missed opportunities because of financial hardships, the missed birthdays and holidays, the missed sporting events and the missed "big" life moments like high school and college graduation, my first job and big successes have molded me into the person that I am today.

I think that you knew that by leaving us alone you were doing the best thing you could ever do for us. Without you, I was able to witness something extraordinary in my life. A mother, a woman who worked extremely hard to take care of her children, do whatever it took to keep us fed, happy and involved and because of that I have become an even harder working individual.

I take nothing for granted and depend on no one but myself to get by, this is how Mom has been functioning for most of her life. Watching this strong, motivated, driven woman will always keep me working towards a path of not only career and financial success but also success as an individual. Helping others, volunteering my time and taking care of me and my family will always be priority.

I don't hold any negativity toward you because I truly believe that you knew, if not at the time, but that deep down you knew that by leaving and completely leaving us be on our own that we would grow into the strong family that you see today.

We are happy and successful and I know that you see that. I hope that you know that you are the reason for a piece of that.

—*AB*

Dad,

As I thought about our relationship at this stage in my life, and what your role as my dad truly means to me, I want you to know a few things. I wish I could say it's been all peaches and cream, and you have been the best dad ever and always been there for me and my brothers, but clearly you haven't. Let me first start by saying you were a great dad from the time I was born until about the age 9. I had all your attention, I was your little girl. We would play in the leaves together, build snowmen in the winter, and you helped me learn to ride my bike. Then I had a little brother that came along, it wasn't about me anymore, which I was fine with. I was so excited to be a big sister and to have a baby brother! When Brad was born he was like any other baby. I loved being a big sister and helping out. The following year Chase was born and I had two little brothers...what more could I ask for?! As Brad got older he started having behavior issues which everyone said was just terrible 2's. It clearly seemed like more, Brad would bang his furniture against the wall, spit in peoples faces, and have temper tantrums like I had never seen. He was eventually hospitalized and diagnosed with bipolar disorder, and put on serious medications that he is still on today. This was difficult for both you and mom, and put a major strain on your relationship.

After I was 8, we didn't have much of a relationship. You were always working, and by the time you would get home you were exhausted and only wanted to relax. Mom was the one that dealt with the domestic stuff, and was who I went to for advice. You and mom ended up getting divorced when I was going into the sixth grade, and it was hard to have much of a relationship with you when I was back and forth between houses. During the week I stayed at Mom's since she lived in Mason and that's where I went to school. On the weekends I was with you, but that's when I wanted to go out with my friends, so I did not really spend any time with you. There was so much chaos at both houses that I didn't want to be there at all. You would get so angry and aggressive and take a ping-pong paddle or belt to whichever one of us was not behaving. I couldn't wait to turn 18 and to leave!

It was hard to hear you and mom bad mouth each other and put me in the middle. It always seemed to be about money, or whose day it was to have the kids. When it was mom's day to have Brad, he would often want to come be with you, his DAD, and you would say no because you did not want to deal with him and say "it's your mom's day to have you." I had to stay strong for Brad and Chase, who it was very hard on. I had to grow up a lot faster than most other kids because of this.

Brad and Chase have wanted, and needed your attention, and you are always too busy for them. That is why I have so much resentment towards you. You have never wanted to acknowledge Brad's mental illness, and it hurts me seeing him hurt because you aren't there for him EVER. Whenever Brad or Chase ask you to do something, you tell them you are too busy. You always seem to be too busy for them, and we know it's just because you want nothing to do with them anymore.

Being a mom now, I could never imagine not being there for my son, no matter what the circumstance may be. I can partly understand why you have not wanted to give them any of your time in recent years, given all the trouble they keep getting into. However, if you truly had been there for them all along, and been a good male role model, they may not have gotten into so much trouble. This is probably the biggest reason I harbor so much resentment toward you. Now that you are on to your new life, with your new wife, and your new house, it seems like you want even less to do with them. But yet you call me and want to see how Blake and I are doing and act as if everything is fine. You want to get together and see your grandson, and always can make time for us, but I think that's only because we don't have problems for you to deal with. Although, even when we do hang out, you are always bringing up how you paid for this or that for Brad or Chase, and still to this day after 17 yrs are bad mouthing mom. Yet mom is the only one still there for them and trying to make a positive difference in their life. You have never once taken any accountability for the way things are, and that bothers me to this day.

After seeing the way my father-in-law treats his sons, I could never imagine him telling my husband that he doesn't have time for him. I wish you could realize all the pain you are causing your kids, but I don't see that happening anytime soon, and for that I am truly sad.

BE THERE AND BE ACCOUNTABLE

What are your thoughts on being there and being accountable?

Be Dependable

de•pend•a•ble

Adjective: trustworthy and reliable

Synonyms: reliable, trustworthy, trusty,

sure, certain, safe

Being dependable is more than just showing up…it's being there when it counts to your daughter, creating a sense of security. When she can't count on anything else, as will happen on occasion, she needs to know she can count on you.

Dear Dad,

Your 70th birthday has given me a good reason to reflect on our relationship at this stage of my life, and on what your role as my dad means to me.

I've thought back over your unfailing presence in my life—the days and weeks and years through which you've fathered like a steady heartbeat—dependable, rhythmic, never missing a beat. I've recounted the million hours of playtime, the thousands of tuck-ins and kisses goodnight, the countless chauffeured car trips. I've remembered the mended broken things and books read aloud and the meals shared. I've relived the moments for which you were there—no matter the sacrifice of work, leisure, or sleep. I've thought about the emails sent from your office and the phone calls made from the car, the advice dispensed in person. I've recalled the hours of grandparenting and home improvements and family dinners that have filled our recent years.

Because Mom and I are so close, I know that on many days you've played a supporting role to her lead; yet there have been moments all your own, and I think you should know what some of them are.

As though it were yesterday, I remember you taking me to buy a car when I was in college. Somehow

I thought this would be a long and careful process, but on the first lot, we found a car we both liked and after a test drive and thorough inspection, you said, "Well, are you ready to buy that car? Let's do it!" Truthfully, I didn't feel ready, and I had no idea how the process even worked, but you walked me through it and by the end of that day, I had a car of my own and the freedom to match. The message was "Leap, little girl. You're more ready than you think."

A few years later, I was living in Atlanta and came home to Pennsylvania for a winter visit. I was training to run a marathon and needed to run 16 or 18 miles in the freezing cold. Mom didn't want me to go—cautioning that my lungs would freeze (or something like that). But you got me out the door and onto the road. I was probably ten miles into that run when I saw your car approaching. You rolled down the window, and handed me a thermos of *warm water*. It was like having my guardian angel appear on that road with just what I needed. You told me where to leave the thermos and said you'd come back to get it. And I was back was on my way, warmed from the inside. The message was "Go for it, little girl. But be smart and well-prepared."

A year or two later, I was broken-hearted after a breakup and came home for Christmas only to learn that a childhood friend had gotten engaged that very same week. Green with envy and convinced I'd never be married myself, I was teary in church during Christmas Eve mass. You took me aside that night, still in the church, held my shoulders, looked straight into my eyes, and said, "Listen to me. One day you are going to fall in love with the right guy and I'll bet he whisks you off to Paris or some other amazing place for the best engagement ever. All in good time." And two months later, I *did* fall in love with the right guy and eventually we *did* have the best engagement ever. The message I heard was "Have faith, little girl. Borrow my confidence until you feel your own."

Two years later, you met me in the back of my church in Atlanta to walk me down the aisle on my wedding day. I remember I had a lot of advice for you about how slowly we should walk and where we should look and how you should hold your arm and then it all flew by in a heartbeat anyhow. We got to the altar and you squeezed my hand and blinked back tears and you couldn't say a word. But the message I heard was, "It's time, little girl. And I love you."

What I didn't notice until I wrote this were that each of these capstone memories occurred during my transition from childhood to adulthood. Each represented a moment when I had to be let go in order to grow into my own life. Only you could have taken the lead in those moments, balancing a mother's instinctive worry and a young woman's fear and enabling me to take the step forward I needed to find my own footing.

Your faith, confidence, and unwavering support have moved mountains in my life. And they have mountains left to move, so don't think for a second that your job is done! Here's to the years ahead, and to playing your part with excellence. I need you more than ever.

Happy Birthday!

Dear Daddy,

I've been thinking about our relationship at this stage of my life and how your role as my dad has affected my decisions and my beliefs and I just wanted to let you know how much it means to me. "You are my sunshine" and "always have, always will" have been my favorite sayings ever since I was little and they mean so much to me. One moment that I will always remember from the second grade at Monfort Heights Elementary is when I went to some kind of assembly during school that involved lots of singing and we sang "you are my sunshine" and I just started crying because it made me think of you. Just knowing that you always thought the world of me has always made me so happy on the inside because when it seems like no one else in the world cares, I know you do. You have taught me more in a short eighteen years than I think you realize. Everything from multiplication to how to change the oil and balance a checkbook—there are many things that I would be lost at if it weren't for you. I also appreciate how you were able to instill in me that "work comes before play" and that when I work hard, the rewards are great. You have also taught me to fight for what I believe in. We are probably the most stubborn people I know and whenever we get into arguments I know it won't be solved over one dinner table discussion. We have gone through all the screaming, the name calling, ignoring each other's existence, until we finally move on. Although these results have not always been peachy or the most desirable, I have learned what values are most important to me and that life doesn't always agree with me. There are also many memories and shared interests that we have that has always made our emotional relationship stable. One of my favorite things that we share is our love for all things chocolate! I know that whenever I go out to dinner with you or I am running errands with you, there is always a more likely chance of stopping and getting a treat along the way. I also enjoy how we share music interests (mostly!) and how we both like to keep up with trending styles. I think I am one of few children that have had the opportunity to see how technology has developed since the 90s because you have always kept up with the next latest and greatest gadget. If it wasn't for your love of technology, I most probably would not be as technologically savvy as I am (even though I still need your help with a lot of stuff)! I also realize that you were not a big fan of dance recitals or dance practice so the fact that you were able to force yourself to come and watch me and drive me all over town really means a lot to me. I have always wanted to dance ever since Mom told me that she was a dancer and she taught Jazzercise, and the fact that you supported me as much as you could makes me feel like you truly care about what I like and what my interests are. As I think about the last couple of months before I left for college I realize that they did not function in a positive or organized manner. There were a lot of ideas expressed about whether or not I was mature enough to go to college on my own. I was not handling most of the stress very well and neither was anyone else and it created a very chaotic household that I tried to avoid as much as I possibly could. I just kept telling myself that when I am on my own things will be different and I won't have to deal with any of this anymore. Nothing in the summer went as planned. But the reality is I don't regret any of it. Everything that happened up to August 16th was purely preparing me for what lies ahead. Sometimes it is good for us to have our space, but other times I really wish that I were with my daddy. There have been many times these past couple of months where I have had no idea what I was doing or what I was getting myself into and I would think about how much I wish you were here with me to help me out. However, I realize that you have done everything for me and have helped me out in countless ways and it's time for me to start figuring life out for myself. Thank you for always being there for me—through thick and thin—and I hope our journey continues to develop in the most life changing of ways. I love you—always have and always will (no matter what!).

Love,
Kelsey

Dear Daddy,

As I think about our relationship at this stage of my life, and what your role as my dad truly means to me, I wanted you to know a few things…

To begin, I would never truly be the person that I am today without you. So much of who I am is because of you and so much of who you are has been influenced by me as well. That is the great thing about our relationship. You have taught me to speed up and work for great things, while I have taught you how to slow down and enjoy the marvelous little things that we too often take for granted. To narrow down our relationship to a tee would be nearly impossible, but describing it through stories may be the best way to really understand.

On December 28th, 1992, I came into this world to change yours forever. Having a little girl is a big responsibility for a man, and not all of them stay around to take care of the ones that should bring them the most pride and joy in life. I like to believe that I had you wrapped around my finger since that winter day. Mom and you took me home to the beautiful house that you built for your family and that is where I grew up. It overlooked a big backyard where you watched me grow and play. The family room is where I remember falling asleep by the warm fireplace on your stomach on a relaxing Sunday afternoon after church and the arms you wrapped me in under your covers after a nightmare would make me feel safe and secure. I can still remember thinking that our house could withstand any storm only "because my dad built it." I think that about many things in life. When you do something, Dad, I feel like it would be impossible to break it. The homes that you've built, the cars that you've fixed and the marriage that you have. Watching how you treat my mother has allowed me to learn how my future husband should treat me. Having the best of everything doesn't necessarily matter; it's the unconditional loving from someone else that is most important.

When I got my first job at fourteen years old, I was washing dishes at a local restaurant. I came home my first night of hard work and said I was never going back. Washing somebody's dirty dishes after a rib dinner was not exactly the dream job that I wanted anything to do with. I swore I would never go back to work there due to the scummy job, minimum wage pay and never-ending heat that would rise into the dish room. It did not take me long to realize that quitting a job after one day of work was not how our family thrived. You said to give it a week. After the week of long hours, sweat and numerous sticky plates, I received my first paycheck. Not noticing how many taxes were taken out, I was pleased and decided it was not that bad after all. I ended up working five years at the restaurant, beginning as a dishwasher and ending as a server. That job bought my car, made myself some new friends and gave me a start on my savings account. Working hard is something I knew I must become accustomed to since in our lives, nothing comes free.

Now that I am away at college, it does create some distance between us. If I need something, you can't always drive two and a half hours just to fix it or to kill a bug. Thankfully you have instilled me with enough knowledge to do what I need to do. You have taught me to fight for what is right, how important hard work is and how to B.S. my way through any uncalled for situation. Thank you for being such a great dad and for supporting me through any tough decision. It was a good thing you married such a wonderful woman though that could instill the compassion and cooking skills that you somehow missed! I love you dad!

Forever your little girl,
Autumn Marie

Dad,

Why didn't you tell me life would go by so fast? Just to think how drastically transformed it is from 5 years ago amazes me. I went from skipping class and finally being legal to drink, to working, home-ownership, promotions, 401ks and my own taxes. Now next year you'll be walking me down the aisle and giving me away to the love of my life, my husband. No tears, Dad, just remember you taught me about loving, and although you're giving me away to the last man I'll ever love, you were the first man I loved.

You have always been the rock in my life, and I've always cherished and valued the rare moments you've given me advice. I think because you held your opinions back so often and let me grow on my own, that when you did give me that glimmer of direction, I saw it as the hidden answer key—my road map. You redirected me before high school to focus deeper on school and achieving scholarships in high school, and you motivated me by committing to me any of the money I saved for college. Not only did this mold me into a straight A salutatorian, but provided me the investment required to study abroad in college. Senior year in high school you saw my passion for chemistry, but challenged me on choosing that for my future major. You suggested chemical engineering and introduced me to your colleagues at work. I would have never known that those few days of advice would afford me my current career starting out 4 levels above what chemistry would have gotten me. Now, I like to call you for your opinion on big decisions, and see how you'd think about it. Recently when asking you about investment options, you didn't reply, but simply asked if I had gotten my fiancé's opinion yet. That was a crazy moment of epiphany, life is no longer going to be about your advice and me, it's going to be about growing and making decisions with my husband.

Dad, I've always yearned for your acceptance and approval, and still do to this day. I remember getting a commission-only summer job and coming home to you shaking your head and saying I wasn't going to make any money. I worked so hard that summer, hitting bonus after bonus, and earning money that would even rival my current career. You were so proud of me and couldn't believe I had it in me. I saved that money and bought my house straight out of college, which also made you so proud. Now, whether it's resealing a toilet, snaking a drain or replacing a fuse in my furnace you continue to encourage me, and I continue to grow, through your affirmation.

You've always been the leader of our family and found opportunities to instill in us the values that were important to you. All of our most memorable family moments occurred on vacations. You always made sure we did 2 big trips a year; one to somewhere warm in the spring and one adventure / road trip in the summer. This was a dedicated time for family bonding. We didn't bring friends, and we didn't split up to do our own activities. We stayed together all day long, just the 4 of us, fishing, swimming, shopping, exploring, eating, or hiking. We shared so many new experiences and bonded tightly as a family. We laughed our heads off in those long car rides and created permanent traditions like the "VAAAACAATIOOOON" chant. That history is influential as I start planning my new life with my future husband, and deciding what values and traditions we want to build our family on. I may have even made him do the chant on our most recent road trip :)

Thank you Dad for building me into the strong, independent woman I am today. Thank you for challenging my dreams and pushing them further. Thank you for taking my tears with my success and always being my rock. Thank you for holding my arm and walking me down the aisle to my future life, and remember your little girl will never stop needing and loving you.

Hey Dad,

A friend of mine asked me to write about the relationship I have with my Dad and how we got to this point. I really feel blessed because even though I know you weren't perfect, you are the perfect Dad for me. Anyone that knows me is aware that I think very fondly of you. One of my guy friends once told me I should not talk about you because it will intimidate any man who tries to get close to me—I say, his loss. I always knew you were an amazing man but it became more apparent as I grew up and interacted with other fathers and their daughters that you are really special. I am not exactly sure what sets you apart from other fathers but when I was asked to write this I started thinking about it and it seems to be as simple as when I needed you, you were always there.

Growing up I put a lot of pressure on myself to be perfect. I am not sure where this came from but it was definitely there and from a very young age. At 8 I clearly remember the time I missed catching a ball to get the other team out at first base. My coach was disappointed and she moved me to the outfield. The outfield at that age meant I wouldn't see any action for the rest of the night. I remember getting really upset and down on myself and you saw it from the stands.

Instead of letting me feel bad about what happened you walked onto the field and you walked me off. You were completely in tune that I wasn't going to be able to move on until I had a chance to compose myself and I think you were trying to prove a point to the coach around allowing kids to make mistakes. Years later other mothers in the stands that day would replay that story for me and how impressed they were with your decision.

What really shaped our relationship through my early adulthood was your support for me making my own decisions even if you didn't understand them. When I came home with my nose pierced instead of looking disappointed you told me it didn't look that bad. Or when I told you at the age of 19 that I wanted to move out to San Diego. You knew I didn't have a place to live and that I was going to be completely on my own yet you were proud of me for taking the leap of faith. I believe I was able to have the confidence to make moves and take risks because at the end of the day I knew that I could fall and you would catch me.

When it came to boys no matter how odd my boyfriends were you never said anything to me that was negative—you just treated everyone with respect.

Maybe you didn't respect all of the gentlemen I hung out with but you definitely respected my judgment. Dad, I want to thank you for being such a big part of my life, for believing in me before I even believed in myself. I want to thank you for treating me as an equal and never telling me that I couldn't do something. If I ever have a daughter I am going to tell my husband to let her make her own decisions, let her fall, let her celebrate her successes and learn from her mistakes. Trust her judgment and don't ever think she doesn't need you in her life.

I love you, Dad!

What are your thoughts on being dependable?

Be Their Hero

Being a hero to your daughter takes everything you have as a dad. But how would you know if you lived up to that billing? Listen carefully to the next few pages. If this is how your daughter would describe you, you're on the right path.

Dad,

I've been thinking recently about our relationship at this stage of my life, and what it means to me. In this reflection, I realized better than just think it, I should write it down and share it with you. So here I go…

You are my hero, Dad. My "Mr. Fix-it House-Project Do-it-All" knight in shining armor. No man in my life will ever compare to what you do with your hands or how good you are at making your visions come to life. I think it's very intimidating and something that most may shy away from. That, combined with what I've learned on my own with home projects and it's a recipe for disaster. I realize that no amount of effort could ever be good enough or "right" enough for me. I will always strive for perfection and may anger those who have put in very good work already. For this, I truly thank you. I wouldn't want it any other way. I can always trust you will have the answer. But, I also know I need to manage this carefully. The male ego can bruise easily where my seemingly innocent expressions or observations can be poorly taken. I need to pick my battles carefully and I need to be OK with not always having the luxury of calling you or asking for the expert advice. I need to know that because you are my Dad, and because I am your daughter, any amount of work will be done in a quality manner.

You are my audience, Dad. I strive everyday to make you proud. I enjoy sharing my stories and accomplishments as they unfold. I have such energy for life and new ideas and activities each day…I enjoy playing them back to you and showing you the good I'm making in the world. And though I know you won't always tell me you're proud of me, I can hear it in your voice. I enjoy making you laugh too. Your soft chuckle draws a huge smile to my face. I picture your squinting eyes and crinkled nose at the sound. I want to bring joy to your life. I know you've worked so hard for so many years…crazy early hours five to six days a week. I know you've been carrying the natural stress of life as well. I just want to be here for you, giving you back energy, encouragement, and strength to face what you need to face.

You are my inspiration, Dad. Life has dealt you some difficult cards, and you've pulled through. You're willing to go through personal transformation (and yes, I'm referring to toupees, mullets, lamb-chops and mustaches) whether self-selected or not. You can push through change, putting up with less-than-ideal while working on the ideal. And once you've made a decision, one that's been logically analyzed and considered, you have the stamina, discipline, and knowledge to make it happen. Life is not dull or broken with you in it.

As I write this, I find I'm writing a wonderful summary of your strengths and your best qualities. I also find my own personal values and strengths reflecting back. Though I may not tell you as often as I should, I admire you so much, Dad. I want so much happiness and success for you in your life. So with this gift of words and admiration, I want to leave three final wishes for you:

1) I hope you can continue improving the world around you: physical, emotional and spiritual. You make great things come to life.

2) I hope you can continue to learn and grow. I hope you continue to read about current events as much as you do today and teach me and others in the process.

3) I hope you can achieve all the things you want to achieve in your lifetime. You have a sense of adventure that comes out every so often...don't forget to feed it.

I love you, Dad. I realize being a parent at any age doesn't happen at any one point, but a summary of points, and that every part of the way you were doing what you thought was best for your family, your kids, and you. I am so proud of you, the man you have become, and the family you've raised. I am so proud to call you my Dad.

Love always,
—kristie

Dear Dad,

It's been said that you never fully understand and appreciate your parents' love for you until you've become a parent yourself. As a mom of two very young boys, I am surer than ever that there is no love more pure, more selfless, more heart-filling and heartbreaking than that of a mother or father for his children. As I round the bend on my thirty-sixth birthday, Dad, I want to thank you for giving me an example to follow in raising my sons to be men of integrity, strength, and kindness.

My life is unfolding now in sinks full of dishes, matchbox cars in the couch pillows, and undereye circles from sleepless nights. Clearly you can empathize! But it's funny—none of us kids ever knew you'd just come off three long on-call nights at the hospital when it was our weekend to visit you. We didn't know until many years later that it was all you could do to keep from dozing off when reading books with us or listening to our rambling stories. What I remember is the energy you mustered for the short two and a half days we were in your hands.

I remember dancing to Elvis songs at Chuck E. Cheese, spending full Saturdays at the zoo or Kings Island, and taking long rides on your old blue and white moped. I remember you donning a gigantic stork costume for the county parade and your patience with me at the museum in Nana's town, where my priority was rushing through the exhibits so I could buy 5cent bubble gum at the gift shop. Hindsight tells me we were three children of divorce staying with their exhausted doctor dad for the weekend, but what's freshest in my mind are the pop tarts we shared and the Johnny Mathis ballads we teased you about when riding in your blue Cadillac. Thank you, Dad, for making Christmases magical and summers postcard perfect. Our day-long drives every June to Callaway Gardens were far from boring. They were chunks of hours to play I Spy and sing along with Michael Jackson and Whitney Houston. And I can't wait to take my boys for rides around the neighborhood to see Christmas lights like you did for so many years. I remember those drives like we took them yesterday.

Our move to Florida meant that you couldn't watch me row at high school regattas, speak at school assemblies, or be crowned queen at the prom. It meant

many holidays spent in airports as we kids made our
way to see you. Your physical absence, though, Dad,
was just that; your big voice and infectious laugh were
right alongside me all those times.

As I've gotten older, I've loved getting to know
the person you were before becoming my dad. I never
tire of your stories about growing up on Littlewood
Drive, hanging out at Teen Town, or pulling antics
in medical school as a card-carrying member of the
"pumpkin procurement committee" on Halloween.
I look at photos of you playing high school sports
or saluting with a smile in your Navy uniform and
think to myself that I would have wanted to be friends
with someone like you. You put people at ease, Dad—
something I'm reminded of when I watch you interact
with grocery store cashiers or take the neighbors' kids
to local football games.

Only as a mom have I come to fully appreciate
that in the backdrop of so many happy memories you
created for me, you were a hardworking dad with three
kids who lived many miles away from you. When my
boys awaken me well before sunrise, and I'm achy and
craving just one more hour of sleep, I think of you and
mom doing the same with three children, and I smirk

in solidarity with you. I am so grateful to now be following in your lead. I can still hear the sound of the garage door and feel your smooth dress shirt on my cheek as we hugged at the end of your workday. I'm immediately taken back there when I walk through the door in the evening and bend down to hug my oldest son.

"Perfect" isn't how I'd describe our relationship, but I don't think there's really such a thing between a parent and a child. I'd say we navigated the bumps of divorce and distance pretty well over the years, and that's more than enough for me. It's now your grandchildren's turn to revel in your fun-loving energy and giggle at the same corny jokes you've told for decades, and I'm pretty sure, Dad, that the only greater joy for me than watching those new memories take shape is being called your daughter.

My love and gratitude to you always,
Alexis S.

Dad,

As I thought about our relationship at this stage of my life, and what your role as my dad truly means to me, I wanted you to know a few things. First of all you are my hero. You have always been my hero since I was a little girl.

There are so many amazing memories that I can thank you for.

Thank you for working so hard. Because of your hard work I got to experience such a great life.

Thank you for taking us on vacations every year. There are so many amazing places that I got to see because of you.

Thank you for all the boats you have owned and the MANY memories that go with each and every one of them. I would not have learned how to fish, ski, tube or have the love for water if it wasn't for you.

Thank you for your discipline. Growing up I hated getting in trouble, I hated when you yelled at me. But I look back on those memories and can only thank you for disciplining me. If you weren't the way you were, I would not be the person I am today.

Thank you for raising me Christian. Because of you and Mom I have a very strong faith in God and I am always thankful for life.

Thank you for being strong. Not just physically, but mentally. The strength you had to have in order to support Mom through her cancer and then fight it yourself is amazing. I was and always will be so proud of the both of you for fighting that fight and staying so strong. You both are amazing!

Thank you for always loving Mom. I admire and love both you and Mom. The love you have for each other is amazing and definitely something I cherish. You have always put her first and provided everything she has always needed. You two are the reason I searched for happiness and did not stop until I found it. Love is contagious.

Thank you for always being there. Reality is that life and growing-up is never perfect. There were definitely times when I thought I could handle everything on my own, but I couldn't. I have been through some really tough times, times when I really needed you to just understand and trust me. The amazing part is you did. Going through my divorce was one of the most horrible times in my life. Not because of the divorce, but because I thought I disappointed you. Becoming an Adult and having to make my own choices about life is scary. At that time I had to make a choice in my life to make sure I provided the best life possible for my son. Leaving a verbally abusive life with a very controlling person was the easy decision, but how to make it through the next chapter of my life and still make you proud was the hard part. And because this is something neither you nor Mom has ever experienced, I was on my own. During that time I made some good and bad decisions that I had to learn from. We all know that I am a very emotional person; I am also a person who will do everything possible to figure something out on my own instead of someone else doing it for me. After my divorce I wanted every decision to be my own, not a decision someone else made. This is the reason I kept to myself and this is the reason I am the strong woman I am today. I know that we don't always agree on everything, but I do know that when things really count, you will ALWAYS be there for me.

Thank you Dad for all that you have done. You are the reason I'm the woman that I've become. It's a pleasure to remember all the happy times we've had. You have taught me to be strong, work hard, fight for what you believe in and live life to the fullest! I am the happiest girl in the world and there's a place somewhere within my heart that only you can own!

Always love you Dad,
Beez

Dear Dad,

Thank you for not only giving me the gift of life, but for giving me the tools, the vision and the inspiration to know how to really, really *live* it…to revel in it, to enjoy it, to be patient with it, to be kind to it, to understand it, to love it, to find the beauty in it, and most importantly, to never, ever take it for granted.

Since I can remember, you've said, "Every day is a gift, kid. Make the most of it." These words are with me every single day. I cherish them along with many other words you've shared, all of which have had a profound impact on me and have helped shape who I am as a person and how I approach life.

The day I got into my car accident the first thing you said to me when I met you in the emergency room, tears streaming down my cheeks, saying that this was the *worst day*, you took my face in your hands, looked me square in the eye and said, "This is the *best day*. You're alive." Thank you for the perspective.

The day I scored my first par, at the exact moment the golf ball sank gloriously into the hole, a bird feather gently floated onto the green. I picked it up and victoriously declared it the 'lucky' feather. You said, "Aim, luck implies you had nothing to do with the circumstance. You're not lucky. You're fortunate. There's a difference. Let's call it the Fortunate Feather." Thank you for helping me appreciate this difference.

The day I first came to you with a challenging work situation I was in 1,001 different directions trying to make sense of it all. You said, "Assess. Adapt. Overcome." Thank you for teaching me the value of focus.

The day I first talked to you about some of my anxieties and what could happen in the event certain things didn't work out, you simply said, "So what?" Thank you for giving me the courage to get out of my comfort zone and believe in myself.

Dad, these are just a few examples. I could fill an entire book. I want you to know how much our relationship means to me. I cherish your words and what they've meant to me over the years...what they continue to mean to me today. And, what they'll mean to my children; and, their children; and, their children's children.

I'm grateful to have you as my father and appreciative to have you as my friend.

Thank you for your unconditional love, your kind soul, and your authentic wisdom. May there be many more happy, healthy, fortunate days ahead, full of life lessons and sincere joy.

I love you.
Aimee

Dad,

As I thought about our relationship at this stage of my life, and what your role as my dad truly means to me, I want you to know something:

You put in the time.

You put in the time to ensure:

…I was loved.

…I smiled and laughed often.

…I grew into an adult with the same values as you and Mom.

…I was armed with skills to succeed.

…I could be anything I wanted to be.

How did you find time to work during the day, sit down at dinner with us at night and cart us around to individual activities most nights and weekends? You didn't just go through the motions; you were involved! I can only aspire to have that same love and dedication with my own children someday.

I appreciate your patience with me. You endured the painful childhood years when I was insistent to quit everything I started. But you figured me out. You found an activity for us to share together. I loved piano lesson days; you and me going to the music studio together to each learn the same art. I also loved listening to you play. I looked up to you; I couldn't wait for the day I would get to play the same songs as you. I wanted to make you proud.

So many people in your life rely on you—to be you. Somehow, I've always felt like a priority (and I'm sure everyone else does too). You make sure the little moments happen. A smile and hug after a great game…or after a bad game. A little laughter in the midst of discipline (because, at the end of the day, nobody was going to die because I got another ear piercing…except for maybe you, if Mom found out that we had a good chuckle about it). A quick hop to your feet to make sure I'm greeted with a big hug when I walk through the door. A wink and an arm tug just before you walked me down the aisle.

If you missed any events in my life, I can't remember them. I only remember you being there. And, for as long as I can remember, I've known that I can always count on you to be my biggest fan.

You've spent so much time in your life being my champion. Recitals, competitions, big games, graduations, award ceremonies, my wedding—all moments where you've shown pride. I hope you and Mom know that those moments were only made possible because of you.

You put in the time.

For that, and a million other reasons, I love you.

What are your thoughts on being their hero?

Love Forever

Love Unconditionally. Be Patient. Be Mindful.
Be Amazing. Be *The* Example. Be There and
Be Accountable. Be Dependable.
Be Their Hero.

Why? So you can Love Forever.

Dad,

Instead of talking to you daily, thanking you for all you've done for me, I thought it a better idea to write you a letter. As I get older I am noticing that my childhood memories are starting to fade, and before they're gone I want to make sure you know how much I love you, even if I didn't always show it.

How excited I was the first time Mom let me walk down to the corner by myself and wait for your car to come down the street on your way home from work! You'd stop, I'd jump in, and it was our special time alone. If I was lucky, it was your night to get milk and we'd pick out some ice cream to bring home. No matter where you went, you always seemed to bring something special home with you. Trips downtown automatically meant fresh doughnuts, but the best were the fresh lobsters from your business trips up east—how much fun we always had sitting on the kitchen floor watching our lobsters run for their lives!

Being the child of an engineer is a special treat— help with homework always turned into an hour long discussion, even if it really only needed to be 5 minutes. Everything had to be discussed and analyzed, pictures had to be drawn and only then did an answer get revealed. Home projects turned into major learning opportunities—the graph paper came out, studious measurements were taken, math formulas were memorized and then finally the project started and the fun began. "Measure twice, cut once", and "check your work" became your mantras and I find myself using both directives continually to this day. You made me a toolbox when I moved into my first apartment, and I think of you every time I have one of those tools in my hand.

College, careers and children brought challenges that you were always there to help with. No matter how many times I fell down, you were always there to pick me up. Nothing got in the way of you being at the kids' soccer, baseball and basketball games, you were the first in line for grandparent's day, and you were never too busy to help them with a science project. You were such a special part of their lives! We still have many laughs remembering all the fun we had together, especially the Thanksgiving that the turkey didn't cook because you insisted the lid did not have to go on the roaster.

Now that you're gone, I miss not seeing you all the time, not having you over for dinner, and most especially I miss the really special times we had together, just you and me. The long conversations, particularly about the early years when you met Mom, joined the Navy, went to college, and started working. All the memories you have given me have kept you very close to my heart. I know you are watching down on me and still taking care of me. I tip a beer (always in a room temperature glass) in your memory. Love you Dad.

What are your thoughts on loving forever?

Your Turn

The following pages are for you. It's your turn to write your own letter. It doesn't matter how long it is, how well it's written, or how perfect you think it needs to be. The value of a letter—to you or the recipient—isn't in those things. The value comes from how much heart is used to do those things.

Dad,

As I thought about our relationship at this stage of my life, and what your role as my dad truly means to me, I wanted you to know a few things...

Thank you for taking the time to pick this book up and read. I hope that you've been inspired and would welcome any feedback you have at my website.

—Clay (www.claybrizendine.me)

Made in the USA
Lexington, KY
30 June 2013